LETTERS TO A
muse

by ERIN FABIAN

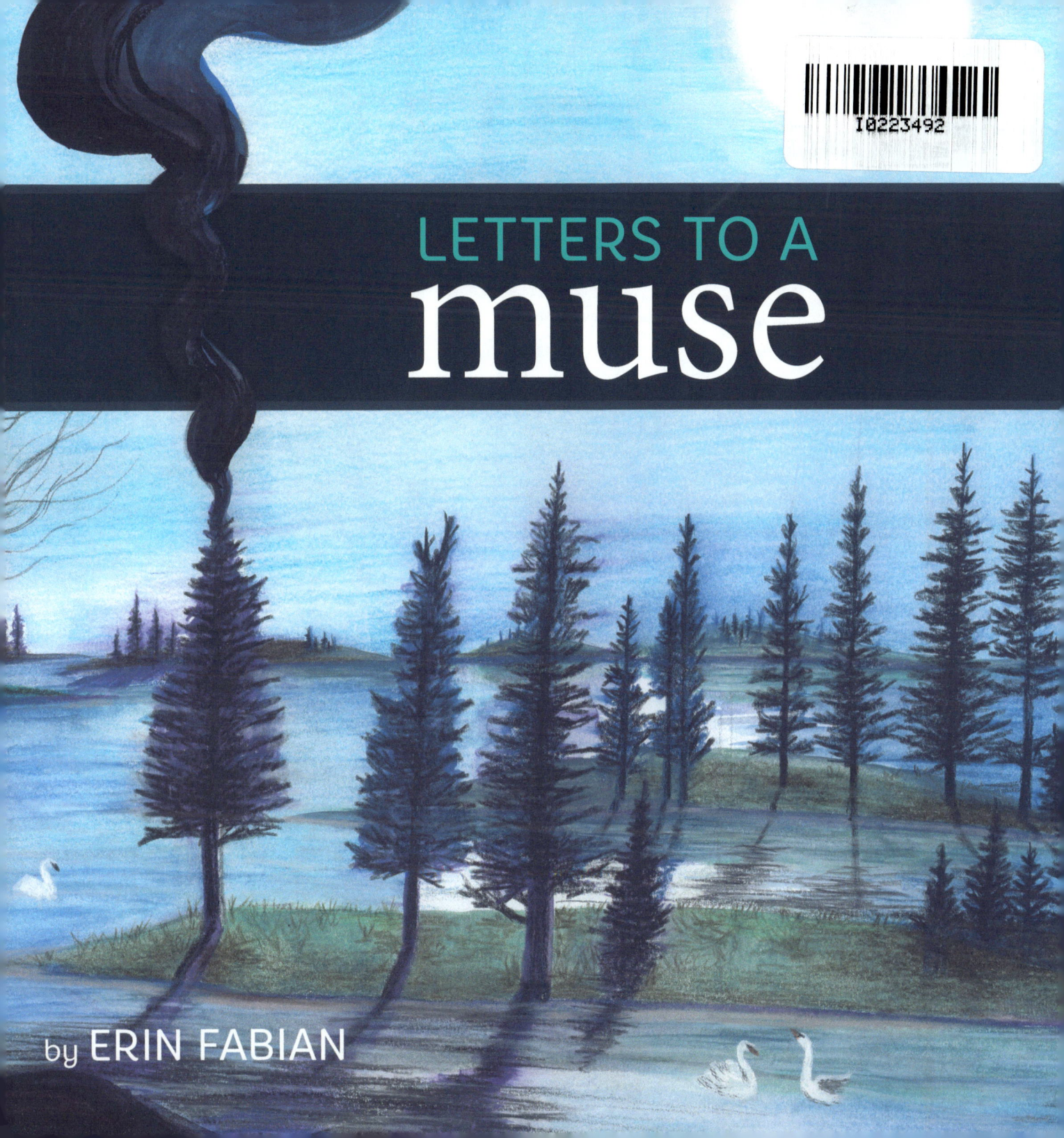

LETTERS TO A
muse

EF

Erin Fabian
2015

EF

First Printing: 2015

ISBN 978-0-578-16644-5

Published by:

Erin Fabian

Miami, FL

Acknowledgments:

GRAPHIC DESIGN AND PRODUCTION:

MARINOFF
DESIGN, LLC

ILLUSTRATIONS:

Lauranda Hook

PRINTED IN USA

Table of
Contents

Prologue

Erin would like to thank her family, her work and yoga colleagues, and her fiancé for all the love and support on a daily basis, which fosters self-confidence, joy, freedom of spirit, desire, and creativity.

She would also like to thank artist, Lauranda Hook, for believing in this collaborative work. It is truly rewarding to produce something authentic, original, and from the heart in hopes of inspiring others to follow their dreams.

> **La belleza y el amor jamás se tiran a la basura. Hay que robarles la vida hasta el último momento.**
>
> —Esmeralda Angüis Sandoval

Introduction

Biography

Erin Fabian was born in Minneapolis, MN and lived in many other cities and countries due to her father being in the U.S. Navy. In college she majored in music and Spanish and went on to complete a Master's degree in Business in Miami, FL. Erin currently works in management but enjoys creative pursuits in her free time, writing, dancing, singing, cooking, practicing, and teaching yoga.

In the first period of writing in Letters to a Muse, starting at about age 16, Erin is inspired by the beauty and harshness of winter, the purity of and fun of friendship, as well as pain experienced from a strained relationship with her mother, which many can relate to in the teenage years. As the years have passed, Erin and her mom have developed a good relationship for which she is thankful.

In the second period which began near age 26, she was inspired by new love and the learning that took place in that relationship.

Finally, the last period of writing began very recently at age 32 after meeting a wonderful romantic partner. This period of writing is the most joyful and is also reflective of the evolution Erin has experienced in her journey throughout life.

As you read through the poems and enjoy the interpretive art, Erin would like that these poems are not only a window into her soul but, most importantly, into yours.

Contemplate your own love and pain, your joy and sorrow, and the beautiful creation that surrounds us daily. The most precious moment we have is now, as we are constantly reinventing ourselves, evolving into more complete beings, perfect in our imperfection.

Some Insight into the Poems:

Erin wrote Chocolate Eyes and Snowcats about her best friend in high school and the memories shared together during daily life as a teenager. Solace, Surrender, and Messiah were all written at times when Erin's faith in God was tested and then God's face was revealed to her in the most humbling moments, allowing her to experience a spiritual rebirth.

In the second period of writing, Erin wrote Silver Moon regarding a very influential person in her life. As she received guidance, she likened this person to the shining, mysterious, and wise moon. Tu Eres, Oasis, and Orquídea Libre were also written about the same person. The reader will notice the metaphors related to nature describing different aspects of that person and the feelings evoked.

Beautiful Girl, Our love, Chanson, Cuando Miro Tus Ojos, and Constance were all written in the most recent period about one very special person. This love inspired Erin to be creative again, to breathe deeply into her own essence, and to fully live and love again.

About the Artist

Lauranda Hook was born in Spokane, Washington the eldest of five children. Her parents were very creative and lived in union with the natural environment of the Northwest Mountains. Hook grew up living off the land and learning to survive in the natural environment. When she turned twelve, her parents decided to escape the harsh mountain winters and relocated to the deserts of Arizona. Both her great grandmother and grandmother were oil painters who inspired Lauranda to start drawing at a very young age. Lauranda has been called a realist/surrealist who has the ability to manifest realities from other times, places, and dimensions into this current time. She went to Upper Iowa University where she studied both education and art from 2003 – 2007. Hook has been teaching elementary art education and yoga for the past six years in Miami.

x

PERIOD ONE:
Circa 1996

Winter

Shadows of fleeting smoke paint across a crystalline canvas

Bright

Shining

Spurious landscape as the trees remain still

Twenty four degrees below zero yet,

as I look outside it seems a powdery paradise

The icicles hanging are like threatening sentinels poised

The sun glistens off each glacial formation

and light is reflected back into the absorbing cerulean sky

The land forms perfect undulations

Each detail of structure, land, and tree

is brilliant and crisp against the vast white

My ears can detect only silence

A silence so profound only embodied in Winter.

ILLUSTRATION: Lauranda Hook

Surrender

I stared into the bleak darkness

waiting for some sign to appear

But nothing came

Not this time

Not the next time

A deep loneliness began to sink in

What would I do without them?

Then I heard angels singing above me so sweetly

They told me it would be difficult and painful

They arose, soaring higher with their voices,

conveying the pain

Then they laid me down gently

Whispering into my ear, comforting me

with their barely audible voices and powerful utterances

"All will be well dear child

The light will always be there for you"

The triumphant absorbing voices completely engulfed me,

sending me across the prism spattered sea

into the glorious Helios

He smiled at me and bade me come in

I gently, quietly drifted into his arms

and saw all I had imagined

My treetops, my silent snowy forest

My cathedral, my valley of wild flowers

It was all there as I surrendered into Agape sunburst.

Messiah

What is that which cloaks us

In purity, kindness, forgiveness

A tangible peace that exemplifies grace

The giver of eternal life

Unconditional love and mercy

Humbler or all, living and dead

Spirit of unsurpassable beauty

Light, solace, sanctity

Peaceful lamb and altruist

Messiah

Solace

Across the balding dusty land

the wind lashes at my cheeks;

Bitter, icy, and scarring

I trudged the eroded land

Searching for structure and finding none

I found a hole and climbed in

Sheltered from the demon climate,

I searched for answers in a desolate world

Lost and empty, my hole provides solace

Serrated arms bleed into the parched ground,

drenching it with panting life.

ILLUSTRATION: Lauranda Hook

Chocolate Eyes

Soft, warm chocolate eyes

melting in candlelight

Rose tinted lips spread into gleaming pearls,

foretelling short ripples of laughter

My face mirrors your contagious expression

The glow of contentment encircles us

as we talk excitedly and share heart thoughts

Understanding each other with just one glance,

my heart ignites with your chocolate eyes!

Snowcats

We pounce in the snow toward one another

Grasping arms in a ferocious hug

We roll and tumble,

our faces buried deep in each other's jackets

Muffling our giggles

Snow flies sticking to our hair and mittens,

we pause to catch our breath,

Scooping the snow and letting it melt on our warm tongues

The cold wind slaps our faces, painting our cheeks pink

We look at each other and smile,

Our heads fly back in laughter

and we fall into the snow together.

Foolish Girl

My salty tears stain my crimson cheek
Why am I so foolish?
I ask into the silence but no answer comes
My soul I always bear
to the object of my unrequited love
My heart left upon the table,
open to all abuse
My naiveté is never realized until it's too late

With each tiny kindled flame,
I treat all symptoms just the same
Doomed to give and n'er to take,
I misinterpret each small deed
to be a product of my need
From this charade I must depart
Foolish girl, foolish heart.

PERIOD TWO:
Circa 2007

Orquídea libre

La orquídea se despierta llena de rocío
resplandeciendo en el sol del amancer
Sus pétalos blancos adornados
    con estrellas rosadas
se extienden hacia el cielo,
    sonriendo al descubrir la libertad

Llegó la primavera, descongelando sus raíces
    delicadas,
entregándole fuerza y vida nueva.

Volando por el jardín, una mariposa se le descubre
    por su diseño inteligente y bello
Su perfume celestial atrae fácilmente
    esa mariposa delicada
Las orquídeas fueron creadas así,
    en un disfraz de olor
Asemejándose entre sí
como una mariposa femenina

Así, dando vida una a la otra
Florecen y crecen juntas
en armonía perfecta ordenada por Dios.

ILLUSTRATION: Lauranda Hook

Tu Eres

Tu eres la sonrisa que me despierta

La mano que me levanta

Tu esencia resplandece y huele a divino perfume

Al tocar tu piel me eriza

Mientras tus ojos brillantes me hechizan

Tu linda boca es fruta jugosa del Edén.

Tu eres la respiración que esperaba toda mi vida inhalar

Estar en tu presencia, escuchar tus cuentos

Me mueve como las montañas

Tan rico es el tiempo compartido que nos bebemos

Suficiente es el conocimiento que mañana nos veremos

Mi luz, mi inspiración, mi paz interior,

Mi amiga, mi amante, mi reina

Mi risa, mi esperanza, mi alegría

Para mi.....Tu eres.

Luna Plateada

Fresca, misteriosa y evocativamente bella
es la iluminación de tu cara
Cisnes flotan como joyas ligeras
en los charcos cristalinos de tus ojos
Estrellas calladas miran de la noche nublada,
parpadeando en tu sonrisa.

Un cervato con mirada fija está en el bosque,
lleno del perfume de pino
Elegante y seguramente se retira
con gracia y su cola clara,
como el movimiento de tus manos.

La arena blanca está abrigada en luz plateada
Un solo camino de energía en líquido se derrite
dentro de las olas oscuras, ondulando
rítmicamente con el viento
que acaricia tiernamente tu mejilla.

Sabia Luna Plateada
Me mira con mirada fija
Tan compasiva y paciente,
como Ella es hermosa.

Silver Moon

Fresh, mysterious, and hauntingly beautiful
is the illumination from your face
White swans float like airy jewels
in the crystal pools of your eyes
Quiet stars peek from the foggy night,
twinkling in your smile.

A fawn gazes in the forest
smelling of rich pine
Elegantly and confidently retreating,
Graceful and white-tailed like the movement
of your hands.

The white sand is coated in silver light
One path of liquid energy melts into dark waves,
undulating rhythmically in tune with the winds
that sweetly caress your cheek

Wise Silver Moon gazes upon me
Compassionate and patient,
as She is lovely.

ILLUSTRATION: Lauranda Hook

15

Oasis

Oasis

Playa desolada
El sol brillante amanece y desentierra aromas
del coco en tu piel de canela
El murmullo rítmico de las olas,
acaricia la orilla mientras escuchamos los gritos sutiles
de las gaviotas al lado

Mano a mano entramos al agua fresca y boyante
la cual se siente astringente en nuestra piel
caliente al principio y despues refrescante.
Nos abrazamos y tus piernas me envuelven
como las enredaderas que ornamentan los árboles
en el bosque

Te me acercas,
tu pecho temblando un poco
la calentura salada de tus besos
contrasta con el mar frío que nos rodea

Nuestro cabello está cepillado por el viento y el mar
Y tus labios apagan mi sed
En nuestra isla paraíso,
se convierte en mi oasis.

Deserted beach
Bright sun rising, unearthing aromas
of rich coconut on your cinnamon skin
The rhythmic hush of waves
caress the seashore as we listen to the faint cry of gulls nearby.

Hand in hand we enter the buoyant, crisp waters
Its freshness astringent to our warm skin at first,
Then refreshing
We embrace and your legs intertwine with my body
Like vines ornamenting towering trees in the rainforest
Your chest close to mine, trembling a little
The warm saltiness of your kisses
contrast with the cool sea surrounding us.

Our hair is styled by the winds and the sea
Your lips quench my thirst
In our island paradise,
becoming my oasis.

PERIOD THREE:
Circa 2012

Beautiful Girl

Beautiful girl so delicate and soft

Your warm skin envelops me like a velvet blanket

The beat of your heart sings my tired eyes to sleep

The caress of your hands is like balsam on my wounds

Each moment with you steals me away

Inside you I see an angel who smiles at me from above

My arms reach out to hold you, keeping you from cold

My body circles around you, loving all your silk

My breath whispers in your ear and kisses your soft neck

My fingers entwine in your hair as you move into my hips

I've never felt so lucky to have perfection touch my lips

With you each moment is eternity, inside heaven's golden doors

We sit upon the clouds together as the sunset falls

Ill never leave your side my love, I'll be forever yours.

Chanson

Tu eres la mujer que nunca conocí
Una sola mirada tuya y de repente comprendí
El tiempo a tu lado llena mi ser
Mi amor te amo tanto, maravilla de mujer

Te amo mi vida
Quiero dormir entre tus brazos
Te amo mi vida
No se que haré sin tus caricias
Te amo mi vida

Tu sonrisa ilumina cada amanecer
Tu cuerpo y tus besos cada noche de placer
Hacerte el amor me lleva al cielo
Completas mi universo sintiendo tu querer

Te amo mi vida
Quiero dormir entre tus brazos
Te amo mi vida
No se que haré sin tus caricias
Te amo mi vida
Te amo, te amo, te amo!

Our Love

Our love is like the vast golden lights of Mexico City; warm, never-ending,

expansive like stars of an ancient galaxy

Our love is like the comforting sand beneath your toes,

massaging every footstep and inviting new life into the body.

Like the mystery of the tempest ocean

and the calm of the rising sun upon smooth waters.

The orange-red and pink hues of a summer sunset

or the crisp bite of fall air walking on crunchy leaves.

Our love is the smell of burning hickory from a hearth in the winter, the frosty fog on the window panes.

Our love is a symphony, the organized chaos of a string orchestra tuning before the first downbeat.

Our love is smoky jazz tune in a dark lounge, lit by candles, a singer crying her passions into the mic.

Our love is the morning sun gently stretching her warm hand across my back,

    casting out all shadows and illuminating my fair cheek.

Our love is a kaleidoscope of colors, bright prisms reflecting light so pure.

Our love...

Cuando Miro Tus Ojos

Cuando miro tus ojos
veo tu sonrisa brillando como reflejo
en charcos de agua clara
Tus labios rojos me confirman la alegría de vivir
Con cada mirada fija, el valor de conocer
Tus brazos extendidos me cantan del amor
y de la harmonia en mi pecho al verte y respirar

Al pensarte me despego de la tierra
y floto en el cielo
Me siento en las nubes y con los ángeles bailo
Tu cuerpo me envuelve con suave piel canela
Ahí me derrito fácilmente y a tí todo entrego
Escucho tus gemidos dulces y tu suspiros
    en el oído,
diciéndome que me amas, así contigo me quedo

Si lloro y mis lágrimas caen en la tierra
Aún en este sitio crecerá un arbol fuerte
y dentro de sus ramas la naturaleza habita

Si lloro y mis lágrimas caen al mar,
las gotas se convertirán en canales que corren,
se montarán en los delfines
para entregarte el mensaje que eres mi amor.

Constance

When I'm with you everything inside me
perfectly aligns
Warmth covers my entire body,
light radiates from my heart
My eyes cannot be stolen from your beautiful face
nor my hands from caressing your body
Loving you is like recognizing myself and my
    purpose in this life,
like finding someone special that I've always
    known is right.

When I'm with you my spirit sings,
 I can't stop smiling and my eyes constantly shine.
When you look at me I see your soul,
deep inside your eyes
I can feel just what you're thinking,
although always a surprise
I love how you care for me and hold me in your arms,
how you watch me while I'm sleeping,
    and keep me safe from harm

Your kisses are seduction
in its purest form
Your lips and tongue caress me
like I've never felt before
I love to be your partner and help you in all things
From the simple to the grand,
I'll always hold your hand.
You're the person who has won me
and conquered my soft heart
I'm going to share my life with you
with hope to never part.

www.ingramcontent.com/pod-product-compliance
Lightning Source LLC
Chambersburg PA
CBHW042012080426
42734CB00002B/53